GIANTS
IN THE LAND

GIANTS
IN THE LAND

DIANA APPELBAUM

ILLUSTRATED BY
MICHAEL McCURDY

HOUGHTON MIFFLIN COMPANY

BOSTON

Library of Congress Cataloging-in-Publication Data

Appelbaum, Diana Karter.
  Giants in the land / Diana Appelbaum ; illustrated by Michael
McCurdy.
      p.   cm.
  Summary : Describes how giant pine trees in New England were cut
down during the colonial days to make massive wooden ships for the
King's Navy.
  ISBN 0-395-64720-7
  1. White pine—New England—History—Juvenile literature.
  2. Logging—New England—History—Juvenile literature.   3. Masts and
rigging—History—Juvenile literature.   [1. White pine.   2. Trees. 3. Lumber and lumbering-History
3. Logging—History.   4. Shipbuilding—History.]   I. McCurdy,
Michael, ill.   II. Title.
SD397.P65A67   1993   92-26526
634.9′8′09740903—dc20   CIP
                     AC

Printed in the United States of America
BP   10   9   8   7   6   5   4   3

To
Jean Crocker Gulliver
who is growing up
in Maine

—D.A.

To my dear friends
Ian and Margo Baldwin

—M.M.

THERE WERE GIANTS living on this land once. Giants whose topmost branches rose high into the air. Giant trees that stood taller than an apartment house twenty-five stories high, taller than the tallest building ever built in New Hampshire or Maine. Giant pine trees that had grown in the New England woods for thousands of years.

In the year 1760 New England did not belong to the settlers who plowed fields and built towns on the riverbanks. It did not belong to the Indians who made trails through the forest and knew where the white-tailed deer came to feed. By law, it belonged to the king of England, George the Third.

King George ruled Massachusetts, Maine, and New Hampshire; he ruled Virginia and Canada, Barbados, Gibraltar, and Bombay. He could rule so many faraway places because England had the strongest navy in the world, a navy of brave men who sailed great wooden ships.

A first-class British warship was larger than Faneuil Hall in Boston. It was larger than the State House at Williamsburg in Virginia, larger than any building in the colonies from Maine to Georgia. A British warship required a mast that was forty inches wide at the base, one hundred and twenty feet tall, and absolutely straight. Nowhere in England did trees grow straight enough to make such masts. In all of Europe there was not a tree tall enough. These giants grew only in New England.

King George sent men with axes to mark his giant trees. Strong men struck three blows, hacking the great, broad arrow of the king deep into the bark. Every white pine that measured more than twenty-four inches across was branded as the property of the Royal Navy.

And then in wintertime, when the land lay frozen and men could not plant or hoe or harvest, they could earn money cutting giant trees. Deep into the woods they went, looking for trees good enough to sell to a king. Not every marked tree would do. Some were crooked. Some were rotten. Most were simply not big enough. But the men kept on hunting, for the king's agents paid good money for mast trees.

When they found trees of the right sort, trees that were tall and straight and solid, the work had only begun.

First, a road had to be cut from the stand of tall pine trees to the river. Mile after mile, over rocks and hills and swamps, the road had to run perfectly straight because a mast tree could not bend to get around a corner. The men cut trees with axes and saws and used teams of oxen to pull the stumps and roll huge boulders out of the way. When the road was finished, they were ready to cut the mast trees.

A tree two hundred feet tall and four feet across had to be cut very carefully, or it would crash to the ground and splinter into pieces fit only for firewood. The men planned the giant's fall so that it would knock smaller trees down as it crashed to earth, smashing their branches to break its own fall. They chopped down young trees and laid them on the ground where the giant would fall, to make a bed of branches for its great weight. Then they hoped it would snow during the night to further cushion the giant's landing.

When morning came, the sound of axes rang through the woods, chopping, chopping, until the giant shuddered, and tottered, and fell. Sometimes the cushioning branches were not enough, or the tree fell in a direction the men had not expected and splintered into worthless pieces. Sometimes the giant turned out to be rotten at the heart. But more often than not the men had done their work well, and a great tree lay dead on the forest floor, waiting to become a mast for the king's navy.

Three pairs of heavy wheels were set on end alongside the great trunk, now stripped of its branches and green, growing top. Chains were wrapped around the giant tree, fixing it to the sturdy axle running between each pair of wheels. More chains bound the top wheels to yokes of patient oxen, waiting for their labor to begin.

At a word, the voices of the drivers rang out in the frozen air—"Huh, Boy, up!" Urging their teams forward, the men worked to pull the chains taut, yanking the upper wheels back to the ground and hefting the great trunk onto the strong axles. With a thud that shook the ground like an earthquake, the twenty-ton tree lay at rest on the three pairs of wheels.

The men breathed sighs of relief and began to unhitch the oxen. One part of their job was finished, and now, twenty yoke of oxen—forty great, muscled beasts—had to be hitched team by team to pull the great mast pine down the new road to the river.

"Hi, Broad," "Up, Bright," "Gee, Boy." The cries rang through the woods as men and beasts started forward along the frozen road. Forward through oak forests naked of leaves and through pine forests white with snow. Forward, straining harder as they mounted the slope of a hill. Cautious, as the lead oxen reached the crest and began the descent, straining at their chains to drag the heavy mast toward the sea.

When all twenty pair of oxen had topped the hill, the leading tip of the mast inched over the crest. On and on it came, the tip straight in line with the rest of the great trunk, until it was so high above the ground where the road began its descent that the chains pulled up and the last pair of oxen were lifted off their feet, bellowing in fright. The mast moved on, steadily forward, steadily higher over the crest of the hill. A second pair of oxen was lifted off the ground, dangling in their heavy wooden yoke. Still the mast came on.

As the center of the great length of trunk neared the crest of the hill, the drivers slowed their teams. Carefully, they inched forward, gently lowering the terrified oxen back onto solid ground.

The cavalcade halted. Teamsters unhitched the lead yokes and took

them around to the rear of the mast, hitching them up again while other drivers stamped their feet and clapped their hands to keep warm. At length the procession lumbered on, oxen in the rear now straining against the great weight to keep the giant tree from rolling downhill too fast.

On level ground they halted again, rehitching the rear oxen back
to the front of the train; the long journey to the river continued step
by icy step. Five miles, ten miles, as far as twenty miles they dragged
the great mast trees, to the banks of the Merrimack and the
Piscataqua, the Connecticut, the Saco, the Androscoggin, and the

Kennebec, the rivers that floated the giant pine trunks to saltwater harbors where the king's men waited to buy them.

The Royal Navy built special ships, mast ships, to carry the great pines to England. Longer than other ships, and deep, with wide doors that opened in the stern to let the giant trees into the hold.

In the spring of 1775, when the news came of fighting at Lexington and Concord, the mast ships were waiting for their cargo at Portsmouth and at Portland, as they had waited every spring for more than a hundred years. But the year 1775 was different. That year patriots towed the masts into shallow water out of range of British cannon, and the mast ships sailed home to England empty. British carpenters had to hammer weaker masts together from the small pine trees of Europe. The giant white pines of New England did not belong to the king anymore.

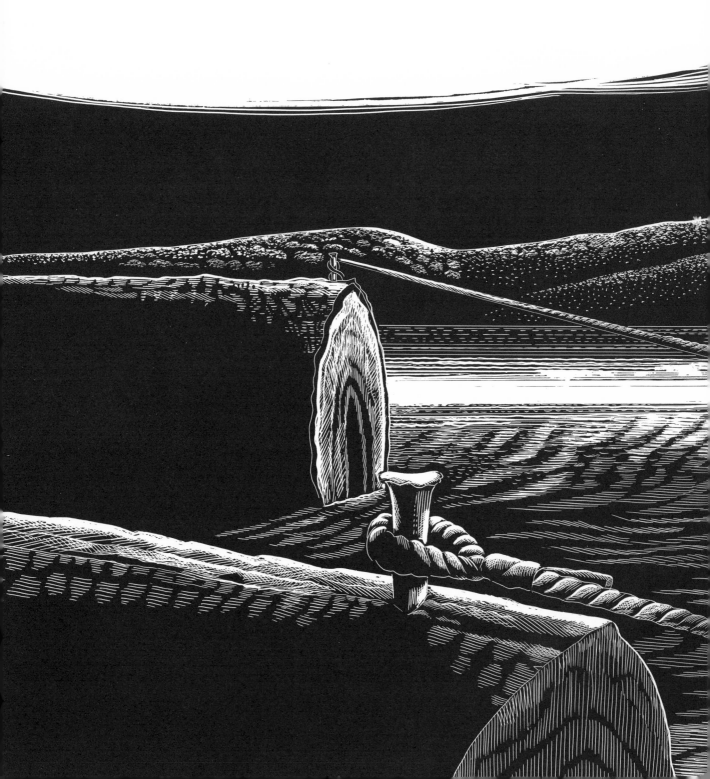

Today one can walk across New England from Mount Desert Island to Lake Champlain and paddle the length of every river from the Machias to the Housatonic without seeing a single giant pine with a trunk four feet across and a top reaching two hundred feet into the sky. They were here once, the giant trees, but those that were not cut for masts were cut and sawn into lumber, or burned for firewood, or chopped into pulp for a paper mill.

But step into the woods on ground made soft by a blanket of pine needles and sniff the air tangy with the scent of pine. Giants are growing.